A TRACT
OF GREAT PRICE
CONCERNING THE
PHILOSOPHICAL
STONE.

PUBLISHED BY A GERMAN SAGE IN
THE YEAR
1423,

UNDER THE FOLLOWING TITLE:
THE TRUE TEACHING OF PHILOSOPHY
CONCERNING
THE GENERATION OF METALS
AND
THEIR TRUE ORIGIN.

A TRACT OF GREAT PRICE CONCERNING THE PHILOSOPHICAL STONE.

CHAPTER I.

ALL temporal things derive their origin, their existence, and their essence from the earth, according to the succession of time. Their specific properties are determined by the outward and inward influences of the stars and planets, (such as the Sun, the Moon, Etc.), and of the four qualities of the elements. From these combined circumstances arise the peculiar forms, and proper substances, of all growing, fixed, and generating things, according to the natural order appointed by the Most High at the beginning of the world. The metals, then, derive their origin from the earth, and are specifically compounded of the four qualities, or the properties of the four elements; their peculiar metallic character is stamped upon them by the influences of the stars and planets. So we are informed by Aristotle, in the fourth book of his Meteor., where he says that quicksilver is the common substance of all metals. The first thing in Nature, as we said before, is the substance which represents a particular conglomeration of the four elements, which the Sages call Mercury, or quicksilver. But this quicksilver is as yet imperfect, on account of its gross and earthy sulphureous nature, which renders it too easily combustible, and on account of its superfluous watery elements, which have all been collected together out of the four elements by the action of the heavenly planets. This substance is composed of a hot sulphureous earth, and a watery essence, in such a way that the Sages have called it imperfect sulphur.

Now, since Nature is always striving to attain perfection, and to reach the goal set before her by the Creator of all things, she is continually at work upon the qualities of the four elements of each substance; and so stirs up and rouses the inward action of the elements by the accidental heat of the Sun, and by natural warmth, that there arises a kind of vapour or steam in the veins of the earth. This vapour cannot make its way out, but is closed in; in penetrating through fat, earthy, oily, and impure sulphureous substances it attracts to itself more or less of these foreign and external impurities. This is the reason that there are seen in it so great a variety of colours before it attains to purity and its own proper colour.

Those mineral and metallic substances which contain the largest proportion of efficacious sulphureous and mercurial vapour are the best; and each quality of the four elements has its own peculiar operation and transmuting influence in such a conglomeration of various substances— their action being roused by the sulphur of the earth and the outward heat of the Sun. Through these agencies the Matter is often dissolved and coagulated, till that which is pure, or impure, is borne upward; and this is the work not of a few years, but of a great length of time. Nature has to purge away the peculiar characteristics of all other metals before she can make gold; as you may see by the fact that different kinds of metal are found in the same metallic vein. This fact may be explained in the following manner. When the sulphureous and mercurial vapours ascend, they are mixed, and united by coction, with the aforesaid substance. If those sulphureous vapours are earthy, thick, and impure, and the heat of the Sun, or their own natural heat, have too sudden and violent an effect, the substance hardens, with all its sulphureous impurities, before it can be purged of its grossness, and it becomes more like metallic sulphur. If the quicksilver is hardened, the whole mass takes the form of some metal, according to the influence of the particular planet with which it is penetrated. For Nature first combines the four elements into some substance or body, which then receives its specific properties through the influence of some planet. Such is the origin of copper, tin, lead, iron, and quicksilver. But it is not essential that I should here describe at length the specific composition and distinctive properties of each of the imperfect metals; they are all mingled in various proportions of impure sulphur and inefficacious quicksilver. Nature, as I said, is ceaselessly at work upon these imperfect metals, purging and separating the pure quicksilver from the impure, and the pure sulphur from the impure, until all their grossness is removed, and they become what God designed that they should be, viz., gold. But if these vapours float upward in their original pure condition, with their inward, pure, and subtle earth, without becoming mixed with gross, earthy, and sulphureous alloy, and if they succeed in breaking forth into the open air, before they become hardened into a sulphureous mass, they remain quicksilver and are not changed into any metal.

If, however, this pure quicksilver floats upward in a pure mineral earth, without any gross alloy, it is hardened into the pure and white sulphur of Nature by being subjected to a very moderate degree of gentle heat, and at length assumes the specific form of silver. Like all the other metals it may still be developed into gold, if it remain under the influence of its natural heat. But if the same pure, unalloyed quicksilver be subjected to a higher degree of natural heat, it is transmuted into the pure *red* sulphur of Nature, and becomes gold without first passing through the stage of silver. In this form it remains, because gold is the highest possible stage of metallic development.

Quicksilver is the mother of all metals, on account of its coldness and moistness; and if it be once purified and cleansed of all foreign matter it cannot be mixed any more with grossness of any kind, neither can it be changed back into an imperfect metal. For Nature does not undo her work, and that which has once become perfectly pure can never become impure again. Sulphur, on the other hand, is the father of all metals, on account of its heat and dryness. In the following chapter we shall refer to this difference, and speak more in detail about quicksilver.

CHAPTER II.

There is, then, in *all* metals true mercury, and good sulphur, in the imperfect as well as in the perfect metals. But in the imperfect metals it is defiled with impure matter, and stands in need of maturing. Hence you see that all metals may be changed into gold and silver, if the golden and silver properties that are in them be freed from all alloy, and reduced by gentle heat to the form of silver or gold. Those metals, indeed, which have been torn up by the roots, that is to say, that have been dug up from their own proper soil in the veins of the earth, can no longer proceed in that course of development which they pursued in their native abode; yet, as much as in them lies, they strive to be perfected.

Now the Spirit of Truth, who imparts all true knowledge, has taught the Sages a Medicine, or Form, by which all the impurities of the imperfect metals may be removed, and the perfect nature, or true mercury, which is in them, transmuted into gold and silver.

CHAPTER III.

But we must now proceed to say a few words about the method of preparing this Medicine, by which the imperfection is removed from imperfect metals through the mediation of perfect mercury, and the mode of gold and silver is developed in them.

I find that the writings of the Sages are all about gold, silver, and quicksilver, which, it is said, must be reduced to the form which they wore before they became metals; that is to say, the form which they wore, perhaps, some thousands of years ago. But the operation of Nature is progressive, not retrogressive. Hence it is a great mistake to suppose that the work of Nature can be reversed by dissolution in aqua fortis, or by the amalgamation of gold or silver and quicksilver. For if the metal be plunged in a solvent, if water be distilled from it, or if quicksilver be sublimed from it, it still remains the same metal that it was before. The specific properties of a metal cannot be destroyed so as to obtain the first substance. Yet Aristotle says that metals cannot be changed unless they are reduced to their original substance.

CHAPTER IV.

What we said in the last chapter shows that Alchemical Art cannot be concerned with the subjecting of gold, silver, or quicksilver to chemical processes. Nevertheless, that which you read in the books of the Sages is most true; and we shall see in the following pages in what sense it is to be understood, that our Art is in gold, silver, and quicksilver. But it is clear that our Art can make no use of quicksilver such as may be obtained from the metals by means of any kind of artificial process, such as dissolution in aqua fortis, or amalgamation, or any other method of chemical purification.

If then, this is not the right substance, or original mercury, it is clear that it is not to be found in the metals. For even if you melt two, three, or four metals together, yet not one of them can give the others any aid towards attaining perfection, seeing that itself stands in need of external aid. And even though you mix some imperfect metal with gold, the gold will not give up its own perfection for the purpose of succouring the other: for it has nothing to spare which it might impart to the imperfect metal. And even if the imperfect metal could assume the virtue and efficacy of the gold, it could only do so at the expense of the gold itself. In vain, then, shall we seek in metals the Medicine which has power to liberate the perfect mercury contained in imperfect metals.

CHAPTER V.

Again, we read in the books of the Sages that quicksilver and mercury are the original substance of all metals. These words are true irk a certain sense. But by many beginners they are supposed to mean ordinary quicksilver. Such an interpretation, however, makes nonsense of the dictum of the Sages. For ordinary quicksilver is an imperfect metal, and itself derived from the original substance of all metals. The Sages, indeed, say little about the *origin* of their mercury; but that is exactly because they use the name of mercury, or sulphur, for the first substance of their perfect metals. If common mercury were not a metal, there would be no metal corresponding to the celestial influence of the planet Mercury, as gold and silver receive their specific properties from the influence of the Sun and Moon. Now, as it is one of the metals, the other metals cannot be derived from it, much less can their properties be derived from it or from themselves, although the real perfect mercury is quite as abundant in mercury as in any other metal. Nor can common sulphur be the first substance of the metals, for no metal contains so much impurity as common sulphur; and if it be mixed with any metal, that metal becomes even more impure than it was before, and is even partially, or wholly, corroded.

CHAPTER VI.

Again, the Sages affirm that quicksilver, or mercury, is the spirit of the specific nature of metals, collected out of the four elements by the influence of the Planets, and the operation of Nature in the earth—and that from it is developed either gold, silver, or some other of seven metals, according to the peculiar effects of the predominant planetary influence.

Hence ignorant alchemists have supposed that all this is true of the common quicksilver, because it amalgamates with all metals, and is soft and volatile. But why should its volatile properties prove it to be no metal? According to this definition, we might deny the metallic character of tin, lead, and other metals, because they do not remain fixed in a fierce fire—though one can stand a greater degree of heat than another. If, again, any substance is to be called the first substance of metals because of the facility with which it amalgamates with them, copper would have a better claim to be so regarded, since it enters into a closer union with gold and silver than mercury, and shares both their fusible and malleable nature. But that is no final union, for it admits of separation; and quicksilver may, with the greatest ease, be separated from the metals with which it has amalgamated. A true union of metals can only take place in the original substance which is common to all. We do find amalgams of three, or even more metals; but then this union was consummated in the first substance, which is *one*, and the whole amalgam would have been developed into gold, if its natural growth had not been retarded by gross, sulphureous, arsenical, and earthy impurity, which is found among metals when purified. The metals which we dig up out of the earth are, as it were, torn up by the roots, and, their growth having come to a standstill, they can undergo no further development into gold, but must always retain their present form, unless something is done for them by our Art. Hence we must begin at the point where Nature had to leave off: we must purge away all impurity, and the sulphureous alloy, as Nature herself would have done if her operation had not been accidentally, or violently, disturbed. She would have matured the original substance, and brought it to perfection by gentle heat, and, in a longer or shorter period of time, she would have transmuted it into gold. In this work Nature is ceaselessly occupied while the metals are still in the earth; but she takes away from them nothing save their superfluous water, and the impurity which prevents them from attaining to the nature of gold, as we briefly showed in the second chapter.

CHAPTER VII.

It is clear, then, that the final union of metals, or their perfection, cannot be attained by the mingling of any specific metals; that the metallic substance becomes useless for our purpose, as soon as it assumes a specific form; but that, at the same time, all metals have a common origin, or Matter, which is one thing, flowing out by the operation of Nature, who ever desires the most perfect form which her own essence and her condition will admit. And this is the form of gold, highest and best of all that belong to the metallic mode. If, then, the purest form of this substance which it is possible for Art to prepare with the help of Nature, be added to the imperfect metals, then it overcomes what is impure in these, for it is not the impure, but the pure matter which is like unto it. But you must not suppose that this power belongs to common gold; common gold has its own specific form, which it is unable to impart to other metals. The power of gold is sufficient only for preserving its own excellence; but our prepared substance is much better and more honourable than gold, and has power to do that which gold cannot do, viz., to change the common matter of all metals into gold.

CHAPTER VIII.

From what I have hitherto said, one ignorant of alchemy might suppose that the teaching of the Sages is altogether false and untrustworthy. Therefore I must now proceed to tell you how it may truly be affirmed that our Art is concerned with quicksilver, silver, and gold, or with quicksilver and sulphur, and in what sense mercury is the spirit of the metals. I will first speak about quicksilver, and at once premise that this word is not here taken to mean that common quicksilver which is one of the metals, but the first substance of all the metals, and itself no specific metal at all. For a metal must have derived its distinctive properties through planetary influences; nor can any one metal be the first substance of all metals. This quicksilver is neither too hot, nor too cold, nor too moist, nor too dry; but it is a well-tempered mingling of all four. When perfectly matured quicksilver is subjected to external heat, operating thereon, it is not burned, but escapes in a volatile essence. Hence it may well be called by the philosophers a spirit, or a swift, and winged, and indestructible soul.

So long as it is palpable and visible it is also called body; when subjected to external cold it is congealed into a fixed body, and then these three, body, soul, and spirit, are one thing, and contain the properties of all the four elements. That outward part which is moist and cold is called *water*, or quicksilver; on account of its inward heat it is called *air*; if without it appear hot and dry it is *fire*, or sulphur; and on account of its internal coldness it is also styled *earth*. In this way quicksilver and sulphur are the original substance of all metals; but, of course, I do not mean that the substance is prepared by mixing common sulphur and quicksilver. The sulphur and quicksilver of the Sages are one and the same thing, which is first of the nature of quicksilver, or moist and watery, and is then, by constant coction, transmuted into the nature of sulphur, which may most justly be described as dry and igneous.

CHAPTER IX.

But I wish to confine my discourse to the quicksilver and sulphur of the philosophers, from which all metals derive their origin; and it is, according to the Sages, a heavy, earthy water, mixed with very subtle white earth, and subjected to natural coction until the moist and the dry elements have become united and coagulated into one body—through the perfect mutual adjustment of all the elementary properties, and by the accidental operation of cold. This is the substance which is used for the purposes of our Art, after it has been perfected and purified by gentle coction, and freed from its earthy and sulphureous grossness, and the combustible wateriness of the quicksilver. It is then one clear, pure, and indestructible substance, proceeding from a duplex substance, exhibiting, in their greatest purity and efficacy, the united properties of quicksilver and of sulphur. In Art the operation is similar to Nature. Hence the Sages have justly affirmed that our Art is concerned with quicksilver, gold, and silver. For in its first stage the substance resembles quicksilver, which is sublimed by gentle natural heat, and purified in the veins of the rocks in the form of a pure vapour, as we explained above. To it we now add silver and gold, and that for the following reason, because we cannot find anywhere else in any one thing the metallic power needed for rousing the sulphur of the quicksilver, and coagulating it, except in gold and silver. For the Sage cannot prepare our quicksilver unless it be first removed from the earth, and separated from the potency of its natural surroundings; and all these natural influences can be artificially supplied only by the addition of gold and silver. Our Art, then, has to find a substitute for those natural forces in the precious metals. By them alone it is able to fix the volatile properties of our quicksilver, for in them alone do we find the powers and influences which are indispensable to our chemical process.

You should also bear in mind that the silver should be applied to our quicksilver before the gold, because the quicksilver is volatile, and cannot with safety be subjected all at once to great heat. Silver has the power of stirring up the inherent sulphur of the quicksilver, whereby it is coagulated into the form of the Remedy for transmuting metals into silver; and this coagulation is brought about by the gentle heat of the silver. Gold requires a much higher degree of heat, and if gold were added to the quicksilver before the silver, the greater degree of heat would at once change the quicksilver into a red sulphur, which, however, would be of no use for the purpose of making gold, because it would have lost its essential moisture; and our Art requires that the quicksilver should be first coagulated by means of silver into white sulphur, before the greater degree of heat is applied which, through gold, changes it into red sulphur. There must be whiteness before there is redness. Redness before whiteness spoils our whole substance.

CHAPTER X.

The quicksilver of the Sages has no power to transmute imperfect metals, until it has absorbed the essential qualities of gold and silver; for in itself it is no metal at all, and if it is to impart the spirit, the colour, and the hardness of gold and silver, it must first receive them itself. It is with the first substance of metals as it is with water. If saffron is dissolved in water, the water is coloured with it, and if mixed with other water, imparts to that water, too, the colour of saffron. Unless the first substance, or quicksilver, is tinged with silver and gold, and coagulated by their efficacy, it cannot impart any colour, or coagulate the (water or) first substance which is latent in the imperfect metals. For it is essentially a spirit, and volatile, and if it be added to imperfect metals, it cannot act upon their water, or undeveloped first-substance, because that is partly fixed by their coagulated sulphur. But if the first-substance has been fixed by means of gold and silver, it has become a fixed and indestructible water; and, if added to imperfect metals, takes up into its own nature their first substance, or water, and mingles with it. By this means all that is combustible and impure in them is driven off by the fire. And herein is the saying true, which was uttered by the Sage Haly: "The spirit (*i.e.,* quicksilver) is not coagulated, unless the body (*i.e.,* gold and silver) be first dissolved." For then gold and silver become spiritual, flowing, capable of being assimilated by the common substance of all metals, and of imparting to it their own metallic strength and potency. And even though this new substance be fusible in the fire, yet, when it cools again, it still remains what it was, nor is it ever again converted into a permanent spiritual substance. It is the quicksilver, then, that constitutes the chief strength and efficacy of our Art; and he that has no quicksilver is without the very seed of gold and silver from which they grow in the earth.

EPILOGUE.

We have sufficiently explained that quicksilver is the first substance of the metals, without which no metal can become perfect, either in Nature or in our Art. But we do not yet know where to look for it, and where to find it. This is the great secret of the Sages, which they are always so careful to veil under dark words that scarcely one in many thousands is thought worthy to find the philosophical Mercury. Many things have been written about it; but I will quote the words of *one* philosopher which I consider as the most helpful: In the beginning, he says, God created the earth plain, simple, rich, and very fertile, without stones, sand, rocks, hills, or valleys; it is the influences of the planets which have now covered it with stones, rocks, and mountains, and filled it with rare things of various colours, *i.e.,* the ores of the seven metals; and by these means the earth has entirely lost its original form, and that through the following causes:—

First, the earth which was created rich, great, deep, wide, and broad, was, through the daily operation of the Sun's rays, penetrated to her very centre with a fervent, bubbling, vaporous heat. For the earth in herself is cold and saturated with the moisture of water. At length the vapours which were formed in this way in the heart of the earth became so strong and powerful as to seek to force a way out into the open air, and thus, instead of effecting their object, threw up hills and hillocks, or, as it were, bubbles on the face of the earth. And since in those places where mountains were formed the heat of the Sun must have been most powerful, and the earthy moisture rich and most plentiful, it is there that we find the most precious metals. Where the earth remained plain, this steam did not succeed in raising up mountains; it escaped, and the earth, being deprived of its moisture, was hardened into rocks. Where the earth was poor, soft, and thin, it is now covered with sand and little stones, because it never had much moisture, and, having been deprived of the little it possessed, has now become sandy and dry, and incapable of retaining moisture. No earth was changed into rocks that was not rich, viscous, and well saturated with moisture. For when the heat of the Sun has sucked up its moisture, the richness of the earth still makes it cohere, although now it has become hard and dry; and earth that is not yet perfectly hard is even at the present time undergoing a change into hard stones, through the diligent working of Nature. But the steam and the vapours that do not succeed in escaping, remain enclosed in the mountains, and are day by day subjected to the maturing and transmuting influences of the Sun and the planets. Now, if this vaporous moisture become mixed with a pure, subtle, and earthy substance, it is the quicksilver of the Sages; if it be reduced to a fiery and earthy hardness, it becomes the sulphur of the Sages. This enquiry opens up the way of finding our quicksilver, or first substance of the metals; but though it be found in great quantities in all mines, it is known only to very few. It is not silver, or gold, or common quicksilver, or any metal, or sulphur. The Sage says: "It is a vaporous substance out of four elements, watery, and pure, and though it is found with all metals, it is not matured in those which are imperfect. Hence it must be sought in the ore, in which we find gold and silver." And when again he says, "If this quicksilver be hardened, it is the sulphur of the Sages," he means that this can only be done by means of gold and silver, which it takes into itself, and by which it is sublimed and coagulated through its own natural gentle coction, under the influence of the Sun's heat, and in its own proper ore.

O heavenly Father, shew this quicksilver
to all whom
Thou biddest walk in Thy paths!